George Newman Bliss

**Cavalry Service with General Sheridan**

And Life in Libby Prison

George Newman Bliss

**Cavalry Service with General Sheridan**
*And Life in Libby Prison*

ISBN/EAN: 9783744760027

Printed in Europe, USA, Canada, Australia, Japan

Cover: Foto ©ninafisch / pixelio.de

More available books at **www.hansebooks.com**

# CAVALRY SERVICE

## With General Sheridan,

### AND

# LIFE IN LIBBY PRISON.

BY

GEORGE N. BLISS.

[Read before the Society, Tuesday, November 18, 1883.]

PROVIDENCE:
PUBLISHED BY THE SOCIETY
1884.

# CAVALRY SERVICE WITH GENERAL SHERIDAN,

### AND

## LIFE IN LIBBY PRISON.

---

It was during the month of July, 1864, that the rebel General Early, inspired with the boastful determination of compelling General Grant to relax his death-grip on Petersburg, marched rapidly down the valley of the Shenandoah with a large force of veteran soldiers, crossed the Potomac, routed the small but gallant army of General Wallace at Monocacy, and pushed on till his skirmishers appeared before the fortifications protecting the Capitol on the west. It was a favorable opportunity for the last rebel raid into Maryland. Great was the consternation in Washington. Riders dashed in from Rockville, but twelve miles away, with the startling intelligence that the rebel army was advancing on the city The government employees were placed under arms, to the great dismay of the clerks in the quartermaster's and ordnance departments, whose knowledge of the art of war had consisted chiefly in sending exasperating suggestions to officers in the field, asking for full explanations as to the loss of some particular sabre-scabbard, saddle or bridle. Perhaps if Early had succeeded in getting near enough to drop a few shells among them, or their papers, it might have had the effect of simplyfying army book-keeping for a time, to the great relief of certain sorely perplexed officers. But it was necessary that something should be done at once to restore that peace and quietness so essential, not only to successful statesmanship in the halls of Congress, but also for the preparation of conundrums by the hard-worked clerks. All this General Grant quietly and successfully accomplished, and rescued the Capitol, without letting go his hold of Petersburg. Among the troops under command of General Sheridan, sent by steamers from City Point on the James River to Washington, was the First Regiment of Rhode Island Cavalry. We numbered about two hundred sabres, under the command of

Major P M. Farrington. Sailing upon the second day of August, 1864, we reached our destination upon the following day, and found that the infantry of the sixth corps had pushed Early back towards Harper's Ferry Marching rapidly through Maryland, we again found ourselves in Virginia, near Harper's Ferry, on the eighth of August. Upon the ninth of August, Major Farrington was ordered to march with the regiment to Middleburg, Va. The real order was to go to Millwood, a few miles distant, but the mistake of a clerk changed it to Middleburg, some forty miles away, calling for a dash through the rebel lines, and a long march through the chosen country of Moseby's guerrillas. About two o'clock in the afternoon the column was in motion, and when the picket line was reached, a sudden dash scattered the enemy, leaving prisoner in our hands, a lieutenant with his horse and arms. This lieutenant was about to be married to a daughter of the citizen in whose house we surprised him. The clergyman was ready to commence the ceremony when we appeared to forbid the bans and take him upon an excursion in no manner resembling a bridal tour. The prisoner was a brave and manly soldier, and bore his misfortune without complaint; one of his legs had been badly fractured by a bullet at Gettysburg, but the injured bones had united without producing lameness. I cannot recall his name, and do not know whether the close of the war left him among the living, but hope that fate was kind, and she was true, and that he was permitted to return and complete the ceremony so rudely interrupted by the chance of war. We pressed rapidly forward, forded the Shenandoah about sunset, near Snicker's Gap, and crossing the mountains near the Gap, bivouacked late at night near Snickersville. At daylight the next morning we were again on the road. A few of Moseby's men were constantly in sight in front, on the flanks, and in rear of the column; but our march was so rapid and unexpected that they were evidently unable to understand what we were about, to get men enough together to offer us battle, or even to annoy and retard our advance. In fact the few skirmishing shots fired were an advantage to us, as they served to keep the men well closed and prevented straggling. At ten o'clock in the morning we marched through Middleburg, to the great astonishment of the citizens, who had little reason for expecting such a visit at that time. Our useless task accomplished, it only remained for us to return to our lines. I was in command of the rear guard, and kept with me two blacksmiths, whose duty consisted in resetting shoes upon such horses as happened from time to time to require such attention. When a horse from the main column fell behind for aid from the blacksmith, the rear guard halted until the work was done, and stopped the advance of the enemy who followed closely in our rear. At such times the blacksmiths never stopped, not even to take a friendly chew of tobacco, light a pipe, or tell a story. The work was done with neatness and dispatch. If they have continued to work in the same rapid and energetic manner in these piping days of peace, they must be worth millions by this time. Late at night, we halted near Waterford, so weary that the men not placed on guard, threw themselves upon the ground and slept soundly until daylight, hardly waiting to unbuckle a sabre belt or roll up in a blanket. Early on the morning of

August eleventh, we rode into Harper's Ferry, having travelled one hundred and twelve miles in less than forty-eight hours, without the loss of a horse or a man. It was known that Moseby had a much larger force than ours, in the country through which we passed, and it was thought at headquarters that we could not escape severe loss, and in fact it was reported in our army that we had all been captured; but General McIntosh who knew us well, said: "The First Rhode Island Cavalry has as many lives as a cat; it will be all cut to pieces one day, and be all right and ready for duty, the next." Upon our return to Harper's Ferry, we learned that our army had advanced, and that our brigade was near Winchester. Moving to the front we passed through Charlestown and Berryville, and camped for the night near Opequan Creek, a few miles from Winchester. About sunrise on the morning of the thirteenth of August, a lieutenant of the quartermaster's department, galloped into our camp with the alarm that Moseby's guerrillas had attacked the rear of the supply train at Berryville, some five miles away At once we were in the saddle and moving upon Berryville at the gallop; suddenly we were astonished by meeting hundreds of well uniformed and equipped infantry, retreating from Berryville, who called out to us as we rode rapidly past them: "That's right, go in, give them h—l!" Major Farrington rode up to the infantry colonel, ordered him to rally the infantry and return at once to Berryville, with his command; the colonel promptly obeyed without, as it seemed, getting it through his head that he ranked any higher than a cavalry major. We reached Berryville with an ample force of cavalry and infantry, but Moseby had seen from afar the whirling dust of our advance. Hastily gathering the mules from about ninety wagons, and such other plunder as could easily be taken, he escaped across the Shenandoah, probably crossing at Snicker's Gap, the same spot forded by our regiment four days before. Although too late for what we most desired, a brush with Moseby, we were in time to drive him away from the larger part of his plunder; fifty wagons with their contents were left unharmed, forty wagons had been set on fire, but we saved eighteen of them, making a total loss of only twenty-two.

Unfortunately, however, the baggage wagons of the First Rhode Island were among those destroyed and with them went all our company and regimental books and papers, and nearly all the dress parade uniforms of our officers. The salutation, "Did you save any of your good clothes?" was a common one about that time, and one officer became very indignant at the statement made by a comrade, that Captain —— had lost, by this calamity, his entire personal baggage, consisting of "a paper collar and a tooth-pick." While giving orders about saving the wagons, I was surprised at hearing explosions like the report of a pistol, followed by the whistle of bullets, and on examination, I found that the fire had reached a box of copper cartridges, and that I was being shot at by a baggage wagon. It occurred to me, with considerable force, that to be shot by a baggage wagon would be particularly mortifying, and I at once gave the wagon the right of way and looked upon its further proceedings from a respectful distance. We found that two regiments of one hundred days' men from Ohio, were in Berryville, as guard for the wagon train, and that Moseby with about three hundred men took a position on a hillside, near the town, and opened fire with a single mountain howitzer, which jackass gun was sufficient to stampede the infantry, and they retreated towards Winchester in disorder, without stopping to fight. There were a few veteran infantry soldiers with the train, *en route* to join their regiments at the front, and they fired a few shots and killed several of the enemy. Only two or three men were killed upon our side, but among them was Jesse W Angell, of troop B, First Rhode Island Cavalry, who was with the baggage train as Regimental Forage Master. He was a brave man and a favorite in the regiment. After a vigorous search we found a black walnut coffin in the village, and buried him with more honor than usually attends a soldier's funeral in war time. The folly of enlisting men to serve as soldiers for one hundred days, and sending them to the front, with officers, (from the Colonel down to the Corporals), entirely unacquainted with the peculiar proceedings of an enemy that used ball cartridge, was never more signally illustrated than by this little incident. Moseby had probably three hundred men, and if there had been a veteran regiment of infantry, two hundred strong, in place of these two regiments of raw recruits, Moseby would undoubtedly have had a pressing engagement to go away from there, and would not have stood long upon the order of his going. The routed infantrymen would have been good soldiers if veteran officers had been in command, or if they had been sent as recruits to old regiments, but the policy so often pursued of raising new regiments to furnish places for officers, without previous experience, cost the country much blood and treasure. The true policy was laid down by General McClellan, at the beginning of the war, i. e. "to keep the ranks of veteran regiments full by promptly forwarding recruits to supply the ravages of war," but, I have sometimes thought, political necessities obstructed the adoption of a policy so simple and yet so wise. The freaks of memory are singular; matters of importance fade from the mind while the impression of some occurrence of little moment remains indelibly fixed. As I write, I recall on that day the form of a soldier stretched out upon the field, stark and cold, with his face turned upwards. A little hole in the centre of his forehead revealed the cause of death, while his empty pockets, turned inside out, gave certain proof that it would be entirely unnecessary to appoint an administrator upon his estate.

For nearly three years I had never been excused from duty on account of sickness, but a week of rainy weather just after this Berryville affair, during which I had the misfortune to be obliged to wear wet clothing in the daytime, and sleep in damp blankets at night, resulted in a strange attack of illness. On the twenty-first of August, as the regiment was marching to the headquarters of General Torbert, to act as his escort, I was forced to dismount and lie down by the roadside, and see the regiment pass on without me. I was finally picked up, loaded into an ambulance, and jolted something over twenty miles into Maryland that night. I remember that I thought one more mile would have killed me. I was sent to McKim's hospital in Baltimore, and from there to the hospital in the grounds of the Naval Academy at Annapolis; at the latter place I met some officers who had just graduated from

Libby prison; they had with them a specimen of the prison corn bread, and the information they gave led me to firmly resolve that I would never allow myself to be taken prisoner. On the eighth of September, although still weak, I rejoined my regiment then lying near Berryville, Va., and by direction of our surgeon, I was treated regularly with his favorite prescription " as much quinine as you can take upon the point of a pen knife, mixed with a somewhat larger quantity of whisky." At this time, Major Farrington was Provost Marshal of the Cavalry Corps; Captain Rogers was Aid-de-Camp to General Merritt; Captain Thayer was Assistant Inspector of the Reserve Brigade; Captain Bliss commanded the provost guard consisting of troops B and C, and Major Turner commanded the regiment.

About two o'clock in the morning of September 19th, the army of Sheridan was preparing for action. General Grant having, the evening before, given him the order he had so often requested " Go in," and in the gray light of early morning the ringing rifle shots gave notice that the hunt was up. As commanding officer of the provost guard, I could see very little of the battle, but prisoners constantly arriving from the front were placed under my charge thus giving me an opportunity for some interesting conversation. A rebel captain, who had been taken early in the morning, confidently assured me, " that we were not going to Winchester." It was a gallant battle, where all our troops did well their part, and as the sun was near the western horizon, a crushing charge from the cavalry corps, well supported by infantry and artillery, sent Early's army whirling in confusion through Winchester, with a heavy loss in killed and wounded, leaving twenty-five hundred prisoners, five pieces of artillery and nine battle flags with General Sheridan. The protecting shades of night saved the enemy from still greater loss. As I neared the outskirts of the town, about nine o'clock in the evening, with a column of eight hundred prisoners, captured by our cavalry, I asked my confident captain of the morning if he thought he would reach Winchester that night; he sadly replied, "It looks like it."

On the twenty-first of September we were in front of Fisher's Hill, which was a strong position, held by Early's army, and it looked decidedly formidable from our point of view. The cavalry was sent to the east up the Luray Valley of the Shenandoah; and next day, September 22d, found a body of the enemy occupying a strong position at Milford; and failing, after half a day's fighting, to force a passage, we fell back without pursuit from the enemy. Upon reaching Sheridan's headquarters, we found that he had been again victorious, and had driven the enemy, with heavy loss, from their chosen position at Fisher's Hill. We were at once ordered to again march up the Luray Valley, in the hope that we might possibly gain Early's rear, and capture a part of his force. September 24th, we again overtook the enemy, who had, unfortunately for them, abandoned their strong position at Milford. General Custer had the advance. A brass band was sent out near the skirmish line, and while they were playing the " Star Spangled Banner," the charge was ordered, and it was an inspiring sight to witness. The enemy left right away, except about seventy captured officers and men, who were delivered over to me. Passing through Luray we forded the Shenandoah, rejoined Sheridan at Newmarket, and marching through Harrisonburg, halted at Staunton, September 26th, ninety miles from Winchester. At Staunton, the Confederate government had large manufactories and storehouses of army supplies. Millions of dollars worth of arms, ammunition, clothing, rations, saddles and horse equipage were given to the devouring flames. The provost guard, Captain Bliss in command, took charge of the lunatic asylum, containing some seven hundred inmates, and gave full protection to all the property of this institution. September 27th, the third division of cavalry with General Torbert, mached about twelve miles east of Staunton to Waynesboro, and bivouacked for the night.

About three o'clock in the afternoon of September 28th, I received an order from Major Farrington to ride into Waynesboro, and give orders to the provost guards to prevent soldiers from entering the houses, as the entire cavalry force was about to pass through the town to water their horses in the Shenandoah. It was a perfect day of early autumn. The clear spring waters and pure air of the beautiful mountain valley had restored me to my usual perfect health. My negro servant, Winson Gaskins, was engaged in frying a chicken, and as I reluctantly turned away from the scene of his promising labors, I assured him that I would soon return. It was five months before I saw Winson again, and my first question was, "What did you do with that chicken;" to which he replied "I thought you was never coming back Massa, so I done eat it myself." I had in my charge about fifty prisoners, taken a day or two before, and as I reached the road leading into the town, I met one of my sergeants with a large quantity of bread, which, under my orders, had been baked in the town for the prisoners. In answer to a question as to what he should do with it, I said, "I will be back in a few minutes and attend to it." I rode into the town, gave my orders, and was about to return, when my attention was attracted by the efforts of a Vermont cavalry regiment to destroy the railroad bridge; the wood-work had been burned, and one span of the iron-work had fallen. A ladder had been reared, and a soldier had started to ascend it for the purpose of making a rope fast to the iron-work of the bridge, so that the men might, by a long and strong pull, bring it tumbling down, when I heard shots in the distance across the river, and looking in that direction saw the enemy about a mile away driving in our pickets; but when the reserve was reached, a charge of our men sent the enemy back again. At first, I thought it was only a trifling picket line skirmish, but soon the reserve was hurled back, and I saw that it was an attack in force. I at once rode to Captain Willis C. Capron, of the First Rhode Island Cavalry, who had command of about a dozen men as provost guard in the little village, and ordered him to form his men in line across the main street, and allow none but wounded men to pass to the rear. This was promptly done, and I was about to return to my squadron, when Captain Capron said to me, "I wish you would take command here, you know I have never been in a fight." At first I refused, but the men looked at me as though they really desired it, and I said to Captain Capron, "very well, take your place in the rear of the line as junior captain," and, drawing my sabre, took my place in front. Our picket line on the opposite side of the river was fighting stoutly, but the force of the enemy was too strong for them, and the firing was rapidly approaching us, when, having rallied about thirty men, it occurred to me that a charge across the river by us, accompanied by vigorous cheering, might produce the impression upon our men and upon the enemy that re-enforcements had arrived, and so check the advance, and give our main body more time to rally for action. It was accordingly done, and with the effect that I had anticipated. I had nearly reached the front when a major rode up to me and said, "Colonel Lowell wishes you to take your command to the ford of the river and stop all stragglers." The order was promptly obeyed, and I was in time to stop about one hundred and fifty men, most of them belonging to a regular cavalry regiment. There were some lieutenants with them, who under my orders, had just about succeeded in getting their men into line, when a rebel battery commenced dropping shells among them, and away they went, sweeping my small force bodily across the river. In the town I again got some of my men together, and endeavored to build a barricade across the main street. It was about half done, when I saw that it could not be completed in time to be of service, and we again fell back until we came to the Third New Jersey Cavalry, drawn up in column of squadrons in the western suburb of the town. Looking again towards the enemy, I saw Colonel Charles Russell Lowell, who had been in command of the picket line, riding toward us with his horse on a walk, the last man to fall back before the advance of the enemy. The Confederate bullets were whistling about him, and frequent puffs of dust in the road showed where they struck right and left of the brave soldier. Putting spurs to my horse I rode forward to meet him, and the following conversation ensued:

"Colonel Lowell, I had but a few of the provost guards, and did what I could with them to help you."

"Well, Captain, we must check their advance with a sabre charge. Is'nt that the best we can do."

"I think so, Colonel."

By this time we had come up to the Third New

Jersey Cavalry, known in the army as the "butterflies," on account of their gay uniforms, and Colonel Lowell said to the officer in command " Major, let your first squadron sling their carbines, draw their sabres and charge." The order was given, "forward;" but not a man moved, they were completely disheartened by having seen the other troops driven back. The Captain in command of the squadron said " Corporal Jones are you afraid?" and the corporal made no reply. The men wavered, and Colonel Lowell said, "give a cheer boys, and go at them," and at once, suiting the action to the words, spurred his horse at the gallop towards the enemy, followed by myself, both of us waving our sabres. The squadron at once cheered and followed. After going a short distance, Colonel Lowell drew out to one side to be ready to send other troops to the support of the squadron, and I was left to lead the charge. I was mounted on a large and strong sorrel horse, formerly ridden by Captain Charles C. Gray of one of our Rhode Island Batteries, and was soon a hundred yards in advance of the squadron; upon reaching the partially constructed barricade I pulled up my horse. Looking back, I saw my men coming on with a splendid squadron front; looking forward, I saw the enemy in column of fours, turning to retreat. The ground was down hill towards the enemy, and I had never seen a better opportunity for a sabre charge, and, as the squadron neared me, I shouted, "Come on, boys, they are running!" and jumping my horse over the low barricade, dashed in among the rebels, only to find myself making the attack single-handed. I had ridden past a dozen of the enemy before I discovered my desperate situation. They were retreating in a loose column of fours, and as I rode in among them there were three files on my left hand and one on my right. I felt that death was certain; and, like a lightning flash, my whole life seemed to pass in review before me, closing with the thought, "and this is the end." There was but one chance; fifty men behind me were shouting, "Kill that d— Yankee!" To turn among them and retrace my steps was impossible; my horse was swift, and I thought if I could keep on until I came to a side street, I might dash into that, and by making a circle again, reach our lines. As I rode I kept my sabre swinging, striking six blows, right and left. Two of the enemy escaped by quickly dodging their heads, but I succeeded in wounding four of them: Capt. William A. Moss, Hugh S. Hamilton, color-bearer of the Fourth Virginia Cavalry, and two others unknown to me. The first side-street reached was on the left. Keeping my head close to my horse's neck, I then broke through the three files on my left, and reached the side-street in safety, fully twenty yards from the nearest horseman. For a moment I thought I was safe, when suddenly a bullet, doubtless intended for me, struck my gallant steed and he staggered under the shock. With rein and spur I urged him on, but it was in vain; he fell with a plunge that left me lying upon the ground. Before I could rise two of the enemy reined in their horses by me, and, leaning over in their saddles, struck at me, one with a carbine the other with a sabre. I could parry but one, and with my sabre stopped the crushing blow from the carbine at the same instant that the sabre gave me a cut across the forehead. I at once rose to my feet and said to the soldier who had wounded me, "For God's sake do not kill a prisoner!" "Surrender, then," he said; to which I replied, "I do surrender." He demanded my sword and pistol which I gave to him, and had scarcely done so when I was struck in the back with such force as to thrust me two steps forward. Upon turning to discover the cause of this assault I found that a soldier had ridden up on the trot, and stabbed me with his sabre, which would have passed entirely through my body but for the fact that in his ignorance of the proper use of the weapon he had failed to make the half-turn of wrist necessary to give the sabre smooth entrance between the ribs. I also saw at this moment another soldier taking aim at me with a revolver. There was only one chance left me: I called for protection as a free mason, and Captain Henry C. Lee, the Acting Adjutant-General of the enemy's force, at once came to my assistance, ordered a soldier to take me to the rear and see that my wounds were dressed. I suppose the soldiers, who were determined to kill me, were friends of the men I had just wounded; but I had no opportunity for obtaining information on that point. A soldier said to me, "Give me that watch," and I surrendered to him the only gold-cased watch I ever owned. Another gentleman said, "Give me your money," and to him I gave my pocket-book, but there was very little money in it; another said, "Get out of them boots," but just then the soldier who had been ordered to take charge of me, arrived, and said, "No you don't; you can't take anything more from this man now, he is in my charge." With some assistance, being weak from loss of blood, I mounted behind my guard; but before I started for the hospital, I heard a soldier say, "It is too bad that horse was killed, he was worth eight thousand dollars." Of course that valuation was in Confederate money. After riding about three miles, I reached a field-hospital, where my wounds were dressed, and I then gave my guard, at his request, my cavalry boots in exchange for an old pair of canvas-top shoes. While this trade was in progress, another soldier, impatient at the generous treatment of the guard, exclaimed with an oath, "If you want those boots why don't you yank them off his feet?" to which the manly answer came, "I do not do business in that way," and he assured me that I was perfectly free to retain my boots if I so desired. I rejoiced that it was still in my power to confer a favor upon one, who, though an enemy, had shown himself to be a gentleman. Later in the evening I was put into an ambulance with Captain William A. Moss, (at that time a lieutenant,) and rode several miles to a small house in the mountains. I found Captain Moss to be a brother mason, who did everything possible for my comfort. He had received a bullet-wound from some other soldier in addition to a sabre-cut from me, but happily recovered from his wounds and now lives at Buckingham Court House, Virginia. My lung having been injured by the sabre-thrust, I had difficulty in sleeping, and the surgeons gave me morphine, from the effects of which I was just dropping off to sleep, when I discovered one of the hospital attendants removing my canvas shoes. I remonstrated, but he said I would be "easier with them off," and made off with them. Need I say I never saw them more? He also, despite my objections, removed my nether garment, giving the same cheerful reason, which, as I was lying upon the floor, near the summit of the Blue Ridge mountains, on a frosty night, without a blanket, did not meet my approval; but I had no veto power and was obliged to submit with as good grace as possible. In the morning my pantaloons were returned to me, but eighty-five cents in silver and the key of my valise had disappeared from the pockets during the night. The reflection that it would be inconvenient for my thrifty friend to steal the valise of which he had so promptly taken the key, comforted me somewhat.

In the forenoon of September 29th, a mounted courier came to the hospital and said he had orders to take me to the headquarters of the general commanding the Confederate force that had attacked us on the preceding day, and that he had a horse for me at the door. I was very weak from loss of blood and told him it would be impossible for me to sit in the saddle, so the messenger returned without me.

Late at night, on the twenty-ninth of September, the wounded were all landed by the cars in Charlottesville, where I was placed in the officers' hospital and passed two pleasant weeks, for a prisoner, thanks to the kindness and courtesy of the officers and attendants, and especially that of the surgeon in charge, J. S. Davis, M. D., Professor in the University of Virginia. Captain Farr, of a New York regiment, wounded at Waynesborough, by a bullet through the lung, was placed in the same room with me. He had received a bullet, piercing the body from front to rear, at Gettysburg, and his recovery from that terrible wound seemed to make him confident that he should survive this wound also, and at his dictation I wrote a cheerful and manly letter to his sister. But the inflammation of the wounded lung steadily increased, and, at the end of a week, Doctor Davis told me that he could not live; and yet he was very strong. At supper-time of the last day of his life he rose from his bed, sat down at the table and ate a large bowl of bread, milk and roasted apples; an hour afterwards he died while apparently in a quiet sleep. I was allowed to attend his funeral, and passing though the grounds of the University of Virginia, I stood by the grave of this brave soldier, and gathering an oak leaf from a neighboring tree, dropped half of it in his grave and enclosed the other in a letter to his sister as the last token from the loved and lost. Through the thoughtful kindness of the authorities I was furnished with a faithful attendant at this funeral, who followed me closely with a gun and maintained a satisfactory state of order in the procession. I might easily have escaped from this hospital had I not given my word of honor to Doctor Davis that I would make no effort to do so. For my benefit, also, an armed sentinel was stationed at the head of the stairs, and on one occasion I found him fast asleep about ten o'clock in the evening. I at once awoke him from his slumbers and gave him a good-natured lecture upon the penalty inflicted by martial law upon a soldier found sleeping on his post. He took it kindly, although he seemed to have a rather vague idea that it was hardly proper for a prisoner to urge his guard to renewed vigilance.

A few days after my arrival at Charlottesville a wounded Confederate from the front called to see me and said he was the first man I attacked in the ranks of the Fourth Virginia, at Waynesboro, and who escaped a cut by dodging. He said, "I tried my best to kill you that day, but your horse was too swift for me; as I followed, your sabre looked like a snake writhing through the air." He said that in an attack upon the rear guard of our cavalry, near Harrisonburg, he had led a successful charge, forcing back at a run, the rear guard, for some distance, until upon reaching the main body the Union cavalry reversed the order of march and pursued the Confederates so closely that, upon coming to a river where the bridge had been burned, the rebels were forced to leap their horses from the abutment into the stream and cross under a heavy fire from their pursuers. My brave visitor said he feared he might be shot in the back, and so turned about and faced to the rear while his horse was swimming across, and a bullet struck his head, plowing a furrow, as I could plainly see, from his forehead several inches back without breaking the skull. As he wore a private's uniform, I asked him how he came to lead the charge, to which he replied that he had been often chosen by his officers to lead charges, and he seemed somewhat surprised when I told him that, in the Union cavalry, enlisted men would not have been thus allowed to take the place and duty of commissioned officers.

While in this hospital citizens frequently came to

see the live Yankee and asked him many questions about what would be done if the Confederacy was overthrown. Although profoundly ignorant, I did not hesitate to give prompt and full information upon all points, and I well remember the indignation with which two gentlemen received assurances from me that the government of the United States would, at the end of the war, take measures for the care and protection (for a time) of the negroes. Although drawing the bow at a venture, I hit the mark, for I described the Freedman's Bureau which was in active operation the next year. One day I had an interview with a lady, apparently about forty years of age. She wore the garb of mourning, and my impression was that she had lost her husband in the war. She was the most eloquent defender of the Confederacy I ever met, and assuring me that God was upon their side, she recounted with enthusiasm the storms that had wrecked our war-ships and troop-transports upon the ocean, closing with a graphic description of "Burnside stuck in the mud." As she paused for breath I seized the opportunity to say a word, and the unequal contest ended as follows: "Madame, if

God is upon your side you must succeed ; if God be for you who can be against you ? and if the Confederacy conquers I will admit that you are right and I am wrong ; that God was indeed upon your side. Suppose, however, that the United States win in the war, will you admit that you were wrong and I was right, and that God was upon our side ?" "No ; that I never will!" she answered, with such spirit and determination as to end the discussion. She had the first and last word, and added one more proof of woman's universal supremacy in a war of words.

At the end of a fortnight my wounds were healed and I was sent by rail to Lynchburg, and confined, with about twenty other officers, in a room where the glass in the windows consisted entirely of iron bars. The first night here was very cold. I had no blanket and laid down on the floor, where I slept until awakened by the cold, when I arose and walked around briskly until I was warm again ; then another nap followed until I was again chilled through. Thus slowly dragged the night away  The next day I began to look around for a blanket, and had the good fortune to find that one of my guards was a mason, who, on being informed of my necessity, told me to meet him at a certain spot in the prison yard at ten o'clock that night, which I did, and received an excellent blanket which did me good service through nearly the whole time of my imprisonment. I had a long talk with my friendly enemy, and found that the blanket, so generously given me, had cost, in Confederate money, forty dollars, which was equivalent to two months of his pay as a soldier He thought that if the good men of the country could have been brought together they might have settled the quarrel without any war. It would give me great pleasure to learn the subsequent history of this true man, but I have forgotten his name and have never seen him since that interview. After another night in Lynchburg, which, thanks to the blanket, I passed in soldierly comfort, we were sent by rail to Richmond. On reaching Burkesville we witnessed the destructive effects of General Wilson's recent cavalry raid. The railroad tracks were torn up so that we had to tramp through the town. As we passed along, a rather rough-looking individual shouted, "Shoot the d—d Yankees!" I turned upon him and said, "It takes a brave man to kill a prisoner." He was shamed into silence, and our guards seemed pleased by the rebuke. The railroad from Burkesville was in a most wretched condition and we jolted along at the rate of eight to ten miles an hour, reaching Richmond late at night, and were marched through the silent streets of the rebel capital to Libby prison. On arriving there, our names were taken at the office, and we were asked to deposit any greenbacks or other articles of value in our possession, except Confederate money, which was not considered dangerous. For our valuables a receipt was to be given, and we were assured they would be returned to us when the time came for us to go North. None of our party had anything to deposit. I am a little curious to know what did become of the money and other articles taken away from prisoners. Earlier in the war, large amounts were thus accumulated at Libby prison from prisoners, and I have never heard of the first fortunate soldier who had his property returned to him upon his release from captivity

While waiting for examination near the office, one

of our men found a barrel of hard tack, and rations were at once distributed, to the great disgust of the officials, who discovered the movement only when the barrel was nearly empty. After our names had been duly recorded a ladder was raised from the first floor to a trap-door in the floor of the second story and we were ordered up. At the top of the ladder we stepped into a room absolutely black with darkness, and were saluted with the fierce shout of "fresh fish!" from a hundred throats. I cannot describe the bewildering and overwhelming effect of those horrid shouts out of the darkness; but it was the usual method of welcoming new-comers to this prison. After the tumult had ceased, we were called upon for such information as we could furnish about the war and the general news of the day, many of the prisoners having been long in captivity. Among them I discovered Captain Edward H. Sears, formerly of the Second Rhode Island Infantry, but afterwards taken prisoner while serving as a paymaster in the navy. Captain Sears told me that in the morning he was going North for exchange, and by the light of a wood fire, in an old box stove, I wrote two letters which he placed in his boot and safely delivered the communications to friends in Rhode Island.

Through neglect, the wound in my body had reopened, and I was placed in the hospital for treatment, where the news came to us of the battle of Cedar Creek. Our first intelligence came through the arrival of about fifteen hundred prisoners, who had been taken during the disasters of the morning attack; but soon we learned from the Richmond newspapers that their boasted victory had been turned into a crushing defeat. To me, the saddest intelligence from the battle-field was the announcement that Colonel Charles Russell Lowell had fallen in the moment of victory Many a time I had looked forward to the pleasure of meeting him and talking over the scenes of Waynesboro, and now he was gone forever; I should never again look on that manly form; never again would he lead to victory the crested line of gleaming steel. Charles Russell Lowell, Jr., was born in Boston, January 2d, 1835. In 1850, at the age of fifteen, he entered Harvard University, where he at once took the first rank in his class and graduated with the valedictory honors. Shortly after graduation he was forced, on account of ill health, to spend two years in travel, most of which was passed in Europe upon the shore of the Mediterranean. His military record shows him to have been among the first to offer his sword in defence of his country Captain, Sixth United States Cavalry, May 14, 1861; Colonel, Second Massachusetts Cavalry, April 15, 1863; Brigadier-General of Volunteers, October 19, 1864; died at Middletown, Virginia, October 20, 1864, of wounds received at Cedar Creek, October 19, 1864.

On the morning of the battle of Cedar Creek, (October 19,) Colonel Lowell, having received orders to make a reconnoissance on the right of our line, set his brigade in motion at half-past four o'clock, and soon struck the enemy in force, thereby saving the right wing of the army from the surprise and disaster that routed our left that morning. Under a sharp fire, Lowell held his position until half-past seven, when he was relieved by infantry, and the whole cavalry corps was sent three miles away, to the left of the field, for the purpose of taking a position to cover the retreat of the army Passing along the fast-retiring line of battle, between the infantry front and the skirmish line, they had an excellent view of the field and were frequently under a heavy fire. "We met everywhere flying men and officers. We asked the officers why they went to the rear. 'They had no command.' We asked the men. 'They had no officers.' They moved past me, that splendid cavalry," wrote shortly after a distinguished general. "If they reached the pike, I felt secure. Lowell got by me before I could speak, but I looked after him for a .long distance. Exquisitely mounted, the picture of a soldier—erect, confident, defiant,—he moved at the head of the finest brigade of cavalry that at this day scorns the earth it treads." Striking the turnpike just north of Middletown, which was already occupied by the enemy, Lowell at once established his position at the extreme left of the line; and he maintained it almost unchanged, against great superiority of numbers, till the final advance in which he received his mortal wound. He attended in person to the disposition of his men, riding again and again along the line of skirmishers, a shining mark for the sharpshooters on the roofs of houses in the village of Middletown. His horse was shot under him early in the day, making fourteen as the number of horses thus killed under him by the enemy In a charge at one o'clock, he was hit in the side of the right breast by a spent ball, which, without breaking the skin, imbedded itself in the muscle and deprived him of voice and strength. "It is only my *poor* lung," he said faintly to the officers, who urged him to go to the rear. "You would not have me leave the field without having shed blood?" The force of the blow was sufficient to collapse the lung and cause internal hemorrhage, and, in the opinion of the surgeons, would have been fatal even if he had received no other wound. For an hour and a half he lay on the ground under a temporary shelter. And now reinforcements had come; Sheridan had galloped to the front from Winchester, twenty miles away, and never yet was a reinforcement of ten thousand men upon the perilous edge of battle so decisive in turning defeat into victory as this tremendous reinforcement of a single cavalry soldier. The order reached Lowell for a general advance along the line at three o'clock. "I feel well, *now*," said he, though too weak to mount his horse without assistance ; but once in the saddle he sat as firm and erect as ever. The color had come back to his cheeks, but he could not speak above a whisper. He gave his orders through a member of his staff, and his brigade, as usual, was the first ready Forward pressed the brigade with its brave commander at its head, and just as they were in the thickest of the fire poured upon them from the town, a cry arose, "The Colonel is hit!" He fell from his horse into the arms of his aids, and was carried forward in the track of his rapidly advancing brigade to a house in the village. His spine was severed at the neck, his body was paralyzed, but his head was as clear as ever. He dictated messages of affection, expressed his satisfaction at the glorious victory, and knowing that for him death was certain and near, he gave complete directions about all the details of his command. His commission as brigadier-general reached him as he lay dying; but as the morning light of October 20th streamed full and clear he was mustered out by death. "We all shed tears," said Custer, "when we knew we had lost him. It is the greatest loss the cavalry corps has ever suffered." "I do not think there was a quality," said Sheridan, "which I could have added to Lowell. He was the perfection of a man and a soldier." In words of truth, glowing with the fire of genius, well might James Russell Lowell sing:

> "Wut's words to them whose faith an' truth
> On War's red tech-stone rang true metal,
> Who ventured life an' love an' youth
>   For the gret prize o' death in battle?
> To him who, deadly hurt, agen
>   Flashed on afore the charge's thunder,
> Tippin' with fire the bolt o' men
>   That rived the rebel line asunder."

But let us return to Libby prison, through whose gloomy portal over one hundred and twenty-five thousand of our men passed as prisoners during the war. Well might it have been written there, in letters of blood, "All hope abandon, ye who enter here." The food given in the hospital was not sufficient to satisfy my hunger, and finding that we were allowed to buy provisions, if we could obtain Confederate money, I made an effort to improve my finances, and finding that Lieutenant John Latouche, the Confederate adjutant of the prison, was a brother mason, I told him my situation and asked for a loan; he said he was unable to help me directly, but would try to find assistance for me. A few days later, Adjutant Latouche introduced to me William F White, a private in a Confederate cavalry regiment, who had recently returned as a prisoner of war from Fort Delaware, and who wished to send to a comrade, he left in that prison, the value in greenbacks of two hundred dollars, in Confederate money, which he gave me and received in return a written order, directing my father to send twenty dollars in greenbacks to White's friend at Fort Delaware. This order was not carried out, my father being unable to find any such soldier at Fort Delaware; but at the close of the war, after considerable effort, I found the address of Mr. White and repaid the loan. Before this money was expended, a Confederate officer came to the prison for the purpose of repaying an obligation. This officer, while a prisoner of war at Fort Warren, Boston harbor, had been visited by a Boston merchant, who gave him fifty dollars, with the request that he would repay it by going to Libby prison, on his return to Richmond, and giving some Massachusetts officer the value of the loan in Confederate money At this time there was but one Massachusetts officer in the prison, and he was in the hospital with me. He was a German by birth, and had come to this country for the purpose of serving in our army; but after receiving a commission, the railroad train in which he was *en route* to join his regiment, was captured by Moseby, and he was mustered into Libby instead. Lieutenant Latouche, wishing to favor me, asked this German if he would give his official receipt for five hundred dollars in Confederate money, and divide the amount with Captain Bliss, which he was very glad to do. On receiving this money, I gave some of it to each officer in the hospital who was without funds, and will say here that during my imprisonment I expended about three hundred dollars in Confederate money for food and gave about two hundred and eighty dollars of the same currency to comrades not so fortunate in getting money One of the prisoners asked me to exchange for paper a two dollar and a half gold-piece, and I induced the Confederate sentinel at the hospital door to give me seventy-five dollars for it in Confederate money This transaction was against the law, and if caught, the Confederate would have been imprisoned; but he probably sold the coin for one hundred and fifty dollars in paper. Our quarters in the hospital, which were on the first floor on the south end of the prison, were very comfortable. There was glass in the windows and the room was well warmed by a large stove. The convalescent prisoners employed their time in playing chess, checkers, cribbage and other games of cards, and also in carving ornaments from beef-bones or other work of similar character. From an old broom-handle I carved a rude set of chess-men, which still remain in my possession as a relic of prison life. For Thanksgiving day a sum of money was furnished by our united resources, so that each of the hospital inmates had generous allowance of beef stew and a large piece of apple pie, the most luxurious repast it was my fortune to enjoy in Libby. The German officer, before mentioned, displayed, at the time of his capture, shrewdness worthy of a native-born Yankee. He saw that Moseby's men were stripping the clothes from the prisoners and giving them ragged garments in exchange, and at once made with his knife numerous cuts in his uniform, and pulling off his boots, cut the tops into strips, from the leg to the toe, so that the plunderers were disgusted with his ragged appearance and left him undisturbed. After reaching Libby, a needle and thread soon repaired the rents in the cloth, while the boots were as serviceable for in-door life as though they had been untouched by the knife.

> "Then why should we grovel for riches,
>   Or any such glittering toys,
> A light heart and a thin pair of breeches
>   Will go through the wars, my brave boys."

My wounds having again healed, I was, on the eighth of December, transferred from the hospital to the regular prison quarters, where I found an old college friend, Captain Henry S. Burrage, of the Thirty-sixth Massachusetts Infantry, who had been unfairly taken prisoner, a few days before, while exchanging newspapers on the picket line. In return for his capture, the Confederate general, Roger A.

Pryor, had been taken prisoner by our men upon the following day, while he was trying to exchange newspapers in a similar manner The next day, December 9th, Captain Burrage was summoned to the office of the prison and informed that he had been selected as a hostage for a Confederate private soldier then under sentence of death within our lines. Captain Burrage reminded Major N. P Turner, the commandant of the prison, that General Pryor was already held as a hostage for him, and that his case ought not to be complicated by this new arrangement. Major Turner admitted the force of this suggestion and examined the prison roll to select another Massachusetts officer, but finding Captain Burrage to be the only one from that State, his eye fell upon my name from Rhode Island, as the next best, and I was summoned to the office, where I was informed that I had been selected as a subject for retaliation. That word struck me then as one of the longest, ugliest and meanest words in the English language, and the revolving years have not softened my prejudice against it. I was further informed that beside myself, Lieutenants Markbreit,

Pavey and Towle were hostages for Privates George P Sims, W S. Burgess, John Manes and Thomas M. Campbell, who, under General Burnside's famous death order, had been tried by court martial and sentenced to be hung for recruiting men for the rebel army within the Union lines in East Tennessee. I was furnished with writing materials and told to write North and save the necks of these Confederates if I had any desire to preserve my own. I wrote at once to Senators Anthony and Sprague, my father and others. The letters were over a month in reaching their destination, but were efficient, as fully appears by the following:

Commissary-General of Prisoners,
Washington, D. C., January 24, 1865.

Hon. William Sprague:

Sir:—In reference to the application of Mr. Bliss, recommended to this office to-day, by yourself, I have the honor to state, that the rebel prisoners inquired of by him, have not been in irons since sometime in September last.

Prisoners of this class on both sides, are, by a recent agreement, to be immediately exchanged. The case of the Union officers, referred to by Mr. Bliss, will be at once communicated to Lieutenant-Colonel Mulford, Agent of Exchange.

Respectfully your obedient servant,<br>
H. W WESSELLS,<br>
Commissary-General of Prisoners.

---

SENATE CHAMBER, January 25, 1865.

DEAR SIR:—I see in the *Providence Journal* a note from your son, Captain Bliss. I received a similar note from him last week, and called upon General Hitchcock, who has charge of the exchanges, and represented the case to him. The General said that immediate measures would be taken for the relief of your gallant son and his companions, and for all others in the same situation.

I wrote to your son, bidding him keep up a good heart, and assuring him that his friends here did not forget him. I write this, thinking the knowledge of it may be a relief to your anxiety.

Very truly yours,<br>
H. B. ANTHONY.

JAMES L. BLISS, Esq.

WASHINGTON, January 21, 1865.

MY DEAR CAPTAIN:—I have yours, dated Libby prison, and have showed it to General Hitchcock, who assures me that measures have already been taken for the relief of you and your fellow-prisoners, and all others similarly situated. I hope you will be relieved before this reaches you; if not, you soon will be, so keep up a good heart and be assured that we do not forget you.

Very truly yours,

H. B. ANTHONY

---

These letters would have greatly cheered us could they have reached our prison cell, but no intelligence from the North came to us. The following paper was given to us three days after our selection as hostages:

OFFICE C. S. MILITARY PRISON, }
RICHMOND, Dec. 12, 1864. }

To CAPTAIN BLISS, LIEUTENANTS PAVEY, TOWLE AND MARKBREIT:

GENTLEMEN:—This is to inform you that you are held in close confinement in retaliation for the treatment received by privates George P Sims, W. S. Burgess, John Manes and Thomas M. Campbell. These men are now held in close confinement and in irons, by the order of your government, at Johnson's Island.

Your obedient servant,<br>
N. P. Turner,<br>
Major Commanding.

P. S.—You can inform your government and friends.

---

Major Phillips was placed in the same cell with Captains Boice and Bliss, Lieutenants Towle and Huff, making five persons in a room about eight feet wide and twelve feet in length. In this cell were two pails, one for drinking-water and the other for slops. It was heated by a small cast-iron cylinder stove, and there was nothing but the floor to sit upon. On the morning of December 9th, Major Turner had told us all that we were hostages for Confederates sentenced to be hung by the United States, and that if the sentences were carried out we should be hung in retaliation. For the first hour after reaching the cell we sat on the floor with our elbows resting on our knees, and hands supporting our heads, in perfect silence, as we thought over our situation. It was indeed a solemn day for us all, and can never be forgotten by those who were there. I can even now recall its horror. We grew more cheerful with the lapse of time, but there was ever the shadow of a possible death by the hangman. No one seemed to care for any game or amusement of any kind, nor was any such method of passing the time ever suggested. We were supplied with a bible and some other books, but the cell was so dark that we could read only a little, and even that often made the eyes ache. In the door a hole was cut the size of a man's head, so that the sentinel, pacing to and fro in front of the cell, could see what we were doing. Our allowance of food was brought every morning for the day There was always a kind of thick soup made of black beans called cow peas; each of these peas had a bug or a worm in it, but we ate the whole, as we could not afford to lose any portion of our scanty allowance. The pea soup was carefully measured out by Major Phillips, so as to give each prisoner an equal share, The Major divided the corn-bread and salt-fish or meat into five piles, made exactly alike in quantity, to the best of his judgment; then one of the prisoners was placed with his back to the food, and the Major, placing his finger on one pile, said, "Who shall have this?" "Captain Bliss," was the answer. "Who shall have this?" "Lieutenant Towle"; and so on until all was disposed of. By this method of distribution all dispute was avoided; but Captain Boice, of New Jersey, made a lively commotion one day by accusing the Major of partiality in measuring the beans; the other three officers sustained the Major, and the Jerseyman was left in a disgraceful minority. Captain Boice told me that he was in command of the squadron of the Third New Jersey Cavalry I led to the charge at Waynesborough; that he wheeled the squadron about and retreated because of a body of the enemy's cavalry on his left flank, and that he shouted to me to come back. Captain Boice was all wrong in this; he should have followed me, and after passing that cavalry force on his left flank, wheeled his squadron about and the flanking cavalry would have found us coming upon their rear, while by that time Colonel Lowell would have had another squadron moving upon their front.

> "But of all sad words of tongue or pen,
> The saddest are these, it might have been."

During the retreat on the night of September 28th, Captain Boice became separated from his regiment and was captured the next day, and thus we met again, in the same cell, as hostages, with a fair prospect of death at the end of a rope, instead of upon the battle-field. For the first time in my life I now fully appreciated the natural repugnance of a soldier to death by hanging. If it was necessary for me to die, while a prisoner, at the hands of the enemy, it seemed to me that I could face death calmly, looking with unbandaged eyes into the muzzles of soldiers' rifles; but I shrank with loathing from the hangman. I often thought of the scenes about the gallows, and firmly resolved that I would not disgrace my regiment or native State if thus called upon to die. I even wondered whether I should be allowed to make a farewell address, and if so, intended to avail myself of the opportunity to assure the rebels that in the future they would again acknowledge the old flag, against which they were then in arms and for which I was to die, as the emblem of our common country. In those gloomy days, I often thought that if good fortune should once more allow me to walk in freedom beneath the old flag, I would never complain under any privations or misfortunes of the future; but alas! these thoughts have not been realized, although the memory of this period has lightened the burden of those trials common to human life.

Our light in the cell came from a well window which had no glass, but was barred by iron rods, and had a roof over it to keep out the rain. As the cell was built of thin boards, with wide cracks, and there was also a hole in the floor, our ventilation was a little too good, and a constant fire was needed to maintain a temperature above freezing. We had a small cast-iron cylinder stove, and each morning the negroes employed about the prison threw in through the hole in the door some logs of green pine wood. They had been sawed the right length for the stove, but had not been split, and were so wet from want of seasoning that they would not burn until cut into small pieces and dried. All we had to cut up this wood was one common table-knife without a handle. Standing a log upon end, and using a brick for a hammer, we drove the knife into the wood near the edge, and then by working with the hands and striking, with the brick, the ends of the knife projecting beyond the wood, split off a splinter some two fingers thick. In this way we cut up all the wood and kept a kind of cob-house in reserve drying about our stove, so that the fuel burning was constantly preparing new wood for the fire. This work was a source of constant occupation for some member of our party, for, as we had but one knife, only one could work at a time, and we kept the cell quite comfortable during the day, but at night the fire of course went out, and sometimes we suffered much from the cold while we were sleeping. Our blankets were scanty and ragged, but we joined them together in making a kind of common bed, and as we laid down, our bodies filled the cell so tightly that if we wished to turn over it was always done by agreement and by word of command, "Ready,—spoon!" at the word "spoon," we went over together. There were at this time nine persons in the cells; Lieutenants Pavey and Markbreit, although hostages with Lieutenant Towle and myself, were not with us, but were in another cell a short distance away, in company with an officer, whose name I have forgotten, and a war correspondent of the *New York World;* though I cannot say for what reason the newspaper man was in there. In our cell were Major Phillips, of Tennessee, Captain Boice, of New Jersey, Lieutenant Huff, of West Virginia, Lieutenant Charles F Towle, of New Hampshire, and myself, and the diversity of opinion seemed to be as great as that of State, for many times there were discussions in which five different positions were earnestly and vigorously maintained. On one occasion the loud talk attracted the attention of the officer of the guard, who, after listening awhile, was heard to say, he "hoped they would rot there." We did not concur in his opinion and he was evidently disgusted with ours. The Richmond newspapers cost us fifty cents a copy, in Codfederate money, but we had one every day, even though we needed the money for food, and eagerly searched for news of the war. One day we read the announcement that General B. F Butler was to command an expedition against Fort Fisher, and for the first time we were all of the same opinion, "that it would be a failure." Lieutenant Huff, of West Virginia, was a huge fellow, six feet in height and broad like his native mountains. In our narrow quarters he was rather an uncomfortable neighbor, and so awkward that if he attempted to move about he seemed certain to step upon us all before he sat down ; but he was a noble fellow, as a little incident fully proved to us. One day a Virginia gentleman, a relative of Lieutenant Huff, came to see him, and the interview was in the cellar, where we could hardly avoid hearing and seeing all that occurred. The visitor, instead of answering Lieutenant Huff's questions about his friends and relatives, seemed determined to insult and abuse him for serving in the Union army  For a time Lieutenant Huff bore these reproaches without reply, but at last his huge frame filled with righteous indignation, and never in my life did I hear more eloquent and patriotic words than those which poured like a mountain torrent upon the astonished visitor, who quickly retreated and left our comrade to be greeted by our unanimous and heart-felt congratulations for his manly defence. Here, as in the other parts of the prison, the vermin called gray-backs, were numerous, and at least once, and sometimes twice a day we examined every article of our clothing, destroying all we could find, whether in the germ or active life, only to find an equally numerous crop the following day. This labor seemed hopeless, but it did keep the vermin in check, for I afterwards saw a prisoner, who, having been either too feeble or too lazy to fight them off, was covered with sores where they had actually eaten the skin from his body.

In the next cell to us was confined Lieutenant H. H. Murray, Thirteenth New Hampshire Infantry Volunteers, and, as only inch boards separated us, we soon arranged one so that it could be slipped out, and thus passed freely from one cell to the other, keeping a good look-out that when the turnkey or any other officer made his appearance, everything was in due form. After some weeks, Lieutenant Towle and myself sent to Major Turner a request that we be put into the cell with Lieutenant Murray, so that we might have more room. This request was granted, and the officer of the guard unlocked our cell door, and we passed out into the cellar and then into the next cell to join Lieutenant Murray with due order and decorum; but when the officer had retired we had a quiet laugh as we thought how often we had been in that cell without disturbing bolts and bars. However, we were now in rightful possession and relieved from the necessity of the former vigilance. This cell was a little larger than the one we left, and I could make three steps forward before making an about face, an exercise I took for at least an hour each day. By our newspaper I noticed that the price of provisions was rising, and I proposed to my comrades to invest our scanty store of Confederate money in rations, which was done, much to our satisfaction, as prices nearly doubled shortly after. We paid for Indian-meal, $1.50 a pound; rice and flour, $2.00 a pound. We bought nothing else, but noticed that apples and onions were $1.50 each, and a stick of cord-wood the size of a man's arm was $2.00, with other articles in proportion. Our guards were members of the Foreign Legion, and all nations seemed to have contributed. There were Irishmen, Englishmen, Frenchmen and Italians. They seemed to sympathize with us, and some of them said, "We are prisoners as much as you, only we have a little longer chain." We studied the faces of the different sentinels carefully, and when we thought, from the appearance of a man, that he could be trusted, we gave him money to buy food for us, which he would do during his four hours off guard, and then bring it to us on his return to the beat. We were never deceived in our judgment in a single case, always receiving promptly the provisions according to the amount of money entrusted to the guard. It was against orders for the guards to speak to us, but most of them did so, although they kept a sharp look-out for the officer of the guard, knowing they would go to Castle Thunder, if caught. As I sat one day looking out through the hole in the door at the sentinel pacing back and forth, he suddenly approached, and throwing a small package into the cell, said, "There is my dinner," and at once returned to his beat. I had not said a word, but like the poor ragged Irishman I suppose my face was "begging with a thousand tongues." Although we bought some food in addition to the prison rations, it must not be supposed we had all we wished to eat. We had an old frying pan in which we boiled rice and made queer compounds of flour and corn-meal; but our rations were scanty and we were always hungry. Some bacon was given us, said to have come from Bermuda, which was the vilest stuff I ever tried to eat. I boiled some of it with charcoal, to disinfect it, but after all could not eat it; my comrades finally forced it down, but I think it must have astonished their stomachs! We employed considerable time in planning methods of escape, but did not reduce any of them to practice. Every night the rats would run about and over us, and the only way we could keep any food was by hanging it to nails driven into the beams over the middle of our cell. One night I awoke to find a large rat sitting on my head, just over my ear, and I sat up on end so suddenly as to throw the rat, like a stone from a sling, violently against the wall of the cell. Judging from the squeal that followed, the astonishment of the rat was fully as great as my own.

About this time we wanted some fresh meat, and Lieutenant Murray turned the full force of his intellect to the construction of a figure-four trap, weighted with bricks, which were to fall and crush the unlucky rat that nibbled the bait. The trap was duly made and set, but the game did not come. The trap was set many times, but I do not recollect hearing a rat move on such nights, though at other times, when the Lieutenant did not have his artillery in position, the animals seemed to be all over and around us. We had much fun out of this unsuccessful hunt, and gave Lieutenant Murray much useless information upon the rat-catching question, and yet were greatly disappointed at the failure, as we would gladly have eaten our lively visitors. I have been informed that there are over two hundred patents on mouse-traps. I hope they will prove more successful than our device. In the cell where Lieutenants Pavey and Markbreit were confined, rats were caught, roasted and eaten, and our comrades assured us they tasted like grey squirrels.

One day as I sat looking out through the hole in the cell door, the sentinel said to me, "I am going to desert next week and go North, and if you wish to send letters to your friends I will take them." I wrote this letter to my old college chum, David V. Gerald:

CELL IN LIBBY PRISON,<br>
RICHMOND, VA., December 28, 1864.

DEAR GERALD:—Before you receive this you will probably have learned through letters written to father, that I am held in close confinement as a hostage, and am depending on the efforts of my friends to secure my release. My release depends entirely on the power of the influence brought to bear in the proper quarter. Such has been the history of the past, and if the means are used judiciously and vigorously, my situation is more promising than that of a general prisoner of war; *i. e.*, I shall be released sooner. There are three of us in this cell; the sun never shines into, it but on clear days there is one place where we can see to read, yet the light is bad and it makes one's eyes ache to read long at a time; the floor of the cell is about two feet above the ground, and we have a little stove and wood enough (so far), to keep a good fire and do a little cooking when we are so fortunate as to have anything to cook. Tell father not to try to send me money, it will never reach me; but he might perhaps succeed in sending me a box with under-clothing, *i. e.*, socks, shirts and drawers, together with some substantial food, *i. e.*, a ham, sardines and onions; onions I especially need to prevent scurvy. I cannot give any directions, however, about these matters, he must ascertain what he can do. I am in good health and fat, strange as it may seem; the rebels have failed to kill me in battle and I don't mean they shall by imprisonment. I often wonder, however, at my escape from death at the time of my capture. I was leading a charge of a squadron of the Third New Jersey Cavalry, and was some forty yards ahead of everything, (I had a very swift horse), when the captain commanding the squadron saw that he was flanked, and was obliged to wheel his men with great celerity and fall back to prevent the destruction of his command; I did not see the rebels on our flank and did not hear the captain shout for me to come back, (which he says he did, for strange to say he is also confined as a hostage in the next cell, having been taken later in the day), so I charged all alone into a brigade of rebel cavalry, who were at the time running away, having been routed by the moral effect of seeing our men sweeping down upon them at the charge; by the time I got among the rebels I became aware of my dangerous situation, but my horse was so much excited that I could not pull him up quickly, and presently found myself so deep among the rebels that it was safer to go forward than back. I expected to die, and resolved to sell my life as dearly as possible, and so made vigorous use of my knowledge of the sabre practice. This was in the main street of Waynesboro, Va., so the rebels were in column of fours and I rode down between their files, and since the rebels had their backs towards me, I went by them like the wind before they knew they had a Yank in the regiment. I wounded a lieutenant, the color-bearer of the Fourth Virginia Cavalry, and two others, total, four; while behind me the rebels were yelling, "Kill that d—d * * * * * !" not an elegant but a very forcible expression. I struck six blows, but two rebels dodged and escaped. At this interesting juncture I thought I saw a chance to escape by a side street, and dashed into it, but at this time one of the bullets that had been whistling about me so merrily, struck my horse, and down he went, and spread me out on the ground. Before I got upon my feet a sabre struck me across the forehead, and I parried about the same time another blow, while a gentleman with a Colt's revolver was trying to get a good aim at me. I jumped upon my feet and said, "For God's sake do not kill a prisoner!" The reb. said, "Surrender, then!" I replied, "I do surrender," and delivered up my arms. About this time something hit me in the back and pushed me forward a step; looking quickly around, I saw that a reb. had stabbed me with a sabre and another gentleman was bringing his pistol to bear. I called out, "Is there a mason here? I am a mason." Some one said, "Are you a mason?" I replied, "I am"; he said, "I will protect you," and he ordered a man to take me to the rear, which was done after I had been robbed of my watch and money, but this was done before the man who was to take me back got to me. The wound in my back was from a quarte-point, and would have been fatal (probably) if the rebel had turned the wrist, *a la* tactics, but his ignorance saved me, since the sabre jammed between the ribs instead of passing smoothly between them. I suffered no pain at all when I was wounded, but had some difficulty in breathing during the first night, since the point of the sabre had slightly injured the lower part of the left lung. When I had a good opportunity to look into my military condition I found five sabre marks on my person, one on the forehead over the right eye, one on the end of my nose, one on the body, one (scratch) on the left wrist, one (very slight) on the top of my head. I was very kindly treated in the hospital and found myself on exhibition as "the bravest Yank you ever saw." I began to think myself one of the most remarkable heroes of modern times, but have now so far recovered as to look on the ground occasionally and talk with my fellow-victims as though I was an ordinary mortal. Once a week we are allowed to go out into the cellar and wash our clothes, which would be a very good thing if I had any clothes. Luckily I had a new suit of outer clothing upon me when captured, so that I am well provided for in that respect; but some of the men here are in such a ragged state as would excite even a miser's pity. About twenty feet in front of my cell a torpedo is buried, and a guard marches with loaded gun forward and back, being specially charged not to allow any one to go near the torpedo; I don't believe that torpedo will ever be exploded. The guards are all foreigners who are pressed into service against their will, and would desert to our lines in a body if they had a chance; they are very friendly and do what they can for us, giving us food sometimes from their own scanty rations. One of them is intending to desert and go North this week, and has kindly offered to take this letter with him. If he gets into a tight place he will destroy it, but if he is fortunate this will reach you. *If you don't get it, let me know and I will write again.*

The military news, garbled as it is by rebel papers, is very cheering to us, and I hope another year will see the old flag waving over this city, and I know that thousands here will rejoice to see it; in fact many have told me so. Please give my respects to Miss ———, and read her such portions of this letter as you may deem proper, omitting the appellation applied to me by my rebel friends. Also, show father this letter. Our rations are by no means sumptuous, but it is possible to sustain life upon them, and when we get something from the guards we live very well for prisoners of war. I have written letters, by flag of truce, to Senator Anthony, Secretary Stanton, Miss ———, father, and the commanding officer First Rhode Island Cavalry. I did not write to you but I sent Ned Sears, Paymaster U. S. N., to see you and tell you the story of my wrongs. Give my respects to your father, mother, uncle and other friends. To make assurance doubly sure, I will repeat to you my military situation: Captain Bliss, Lieutenants Markbreit, Pavey and Towle, are held as hostages for

Privates George P. Sims, W S. Burgess, John Manes and Thomas M. Campbell, C. S. Army, now confined in irons at Johnson's Island, Ohio, by the United States. When they are released and sent South we shall be sent North. There are ten hostages (all in the entire South) confined here, four in one cell, and three in each of the other two.

This is a tight place, but I have seen a great many narrow places in safety before, and hope we may meet again,

> "With freedom's soil beneath our feet,
> And freedom's banner streaming o'er us."

Yours truly,

G. N. BLISS.

---

This letter reached its destination, accompanied by the following from a gallant Rhode Island naval officer:

U S. STEAMER, COMMANDER READ,
RAPPAHANNOCK RIVER, VA., March 10, 1865.

FRIEND GERALD:

DEAR SIR:—I enclose herewith a letter from our mutual friend, Captain Bliss. I received it at the hands of a deserter from the rebel army, whom I picked up about one hundred miles up the river, and whom I have sent North. Hoping we may soon have the pleasure of greeting our friend again, I remain,

Very respectfully your obedient servant,<br>
EDWARD HOOKER,<br>
Lieutenant-Commander, U. S. N

---

Soon after writing this letter, the hardships of prison life placed me upon the sick list, and the medicine given me by the Confederate surgeon seemed to do no good, and indeed it would have been surprising if the mere taking of drugs could have availed against the constant pressure of our unhealthy life and surroundings. My comrades would talk for hours over detailed descriptions of banquets which they had enjoyed in that Northern land, always called "God's Country" by prisoners, and would go over elaborate bills of fare, filled with dainties, which they proposed to feast upon when again so fortunate as to breathe free air. These efforts of memory or imagination were to me an aggravation of the miseries we endured, but my earnest protests had no effect upon my fellow-prisoners. For myself, I carefully avoided, so far as possible, all thoughts of home, friends and the comforts of civilization, finding in such indulgences a mental excitement that warned me "that way madness lies." At night, one of our number would cut a notch upon the edge of a board and say, "Another day of misery gone." Thus the long, dreary days wore on until January 25, 1865, when we were surprised by orders to leave the cells and return to our former quarters in the second story of the building. No explanation or information whatever was given us for the change, but we guessed, of course, that some arrangement had been made for the exchange of hostages. I was still sick, and remained only one night here before being returned to my old place in the hospital, where I found nearly all the comrades I had left there December 8, 1864. Although sick, I was able to eat all the rations allowed prisoners and four dollars' worth of white bread each day; but flour was nine hundred dollars a barrel and bread was one dollar a loaf, so that the four loaves together were only about the size of a man's fist. This was the price in paper, but in silver, flour was only six dollars a barrel.

On the morning of February 5, 1865, Ross, the clerk of the prison, brought me a parole roll, which I signed, promising to do no harm to the Confederacy until duly exchanged and passed out of Libby prison into the streets of Richmond. In less than two months from this day, colored troops of the Union army were marching through the city and the Confederacy was without a capital. A few days later, President Lincoln visited the city. He made a brief call at Libby prison, breathed for a moment its tainted air, gazed upon its grated windows, trod the slimy floors, and was deeply moved at the reflection of the horrors thus recalled. Joining the procession of my fellow-hostages and several hundred enlisted men, we marched half a mile down the river bank, and then on board a small steamer, and sailed down the James river We passed through the vessels of the Confederate navy. They had the appearance of large steam-tugs, furnished with powerful torpedoes carried upon long projecting poles at the bows. We landed near Dutch Gap, and marched across the neck of land to the steamer "New York," over which the old flag was waving, and a band of music welcomed us with the sweet strains of "Home, sweet home." I wish I could describe the scenes which followed among that happy company of released prisoners; men were dancing, shouting, singing, rolling on the ground, and some were shedding tears for very joy; any one ignorant of the fact that we were released prisoners of war, would surely have thought we were all *drunk,*—and so indeed we were, intoxicated with joy The excitement was so great that there was hardly any sleep among those happy men for the first forty-eight hours of freedom. There seemed to be a universal desire among them to give some one who had never been a prisoner a full account of life under the Confederate flag, and I noticed many men held as the "Ancient Mariner" held the wedding guest.

On the morning of February 7th, our steamer landed us at Annapolis, Maryland, and I sent to D. V Gerald, Providence, the following telegram:

"Out of the horrible pit and miry clay Tell father."

Four months of prison life had broken my health more than the previous three years of hardship and exposure in the army. When exchanged, I was placed on light duty as president of a court martial at Annapolis, Maryland, and May 15, 1865, was mustered out of service and returned to peaceful life in my native State of Rhode Island.

# APPENDIX

There was seldom any personal bitterness between the brave soldiers, who, in the Union and Confederate armies, so often met in battle, and many of our former foes have now warm friends among the Union veterans. Since the war, I have had the pleasure of revisiting, many times, old scenes in Virginia, and meeting soldiers who fought on the other side. Said a civilian recently, as he saw the cordiality between our comrades and their Southern guests, "And these are the men our soldiers were trying to lick a few years ago, and now see how they respect them!" And an old veteran replied, "Hang it, sir, *you'd* respect 'em if you'd *been there* and seen how hard they were to lick!"

The following have the merit of being personal narratives, and are therefore here given in print:

# APPENDIX.

A NARRATIVE *of a Part of the Operations of the Confederate Cavalry in the Valley of the Shenandoah, Va., During the Autumn of 1864:*

After the disastrous day at Winchester, on the 19th of September, 1864, the cavalry force attached to General Jubal A. Early's command, consisting of one division (Fitz Lee's) composed of Lomax's brigade, commanded by General William H. Payne, and Wickham's brigade, under the command of Colonel Thomas T. Munford, all commanded by General Williams C. Wickham; Fitz Lee having been wounded and disabled at Winchester, fell back to Front Royal, and attempted to guard the fords of the Shenandoah river at that point. They were pursued by a superior force of the enemy, who, masking their real design by a feint upon the front of the river line, occupied by the Confederate cavalry, succeeded in crossing at an unguarded ford, and compelled an abandonment of the position by the Confederates. It will be observed that the army of General Early was at this time retreating on two parallel lines, the infantry down the Shenandoah valley proper, and the cavalry down what is called the Page valley, formed by the Blue Ridge mountains and the Massanuttin mountains, a spur of the Blue Ridge. It was evidently the object of the Union cavalry, by this flank movement, to get in rear of General Early's main army and thus inclose him between two forces, General Sheridan, with his infantry force and part of his cavalry being in his front. The Confederate cavalry endeavored to prevent this by retreating and obstructing the advance of the Union cavalry force in their front, until General Early could reach a place where this purpose could not be accomplished. General Wickham, in furtherance of this design, fell back slowly with his division down the Page valley, disputing the advance of the enemy, and reached Brown Gap, a pass in the Blue Ridge, in Augusta county, on the 26th day of September. Early, by this time, had reached what was supposed to be a defensible position from a flank and rear attack. While Wickham was encamped at Brown's Gap, information was received by the Confederates that a small Union cavalry force was outlying at or near the village of Waynesboro, in Augusta county, situated on the railroad from Charlottesville to Staunton, and near the mouth of Rockfish Gap. It was believed that this force was unsupported by infantry, and by a swift and bold attack by the Confederates, could be captured or severely crippled. Accordingly, on the morning of the 28th of September,

Wickham's brigade of cavalry, commanded by Colonel Munford, consisting of the First, Second, Third and Fourth Regiments of Virginia cavalry, with a section of horse artillery, moved upon Waynesboro, and at the same time, General John C. Breckenridge's division of infantry was put in motion down the valley pike to strike the road from Waynesboro to Staunton, at some point that would intercept the retreat of the Union cavalry. Colonel Munford, with his cavalry, wound along the base of the Blue Ridge, on the west side, by obscure mountain roads, as noiselessly and swiftly as possible, reaching the Charlottesville and Waynesboro road, about a mile from the village, at four o'clock of the afternoon of the 28th of September. As was hoped, the enemy were completely surprised; many of their horses were unbridled and grazing on a piece of meadowland lying between the highway leading to the village and a small stream, a tributary of the South river, one of the branches of the Shenandoah. Colonel Munford, as soon as he saw the situation, quietly disposed his forces for an attack; the First Regiment, commanded by Colonel Willy Carter, was dismounted as sharpshooters, and formed on either side of the road leading to Waynesboro, and the remaining three regiments advanced quietly upon the village, mounted. The enemy immediately began to bestir themselves, and in a few minutes their cavalry made its appearance in front of the village, between it and the Confederates. A sharp engagement at once ensued; charges and counter-charges were made by the opposing forces, but the Union cavalry was forced steadily back into and through the village, until the western edge was reached, where the Confederates found some obstructions across the street, doubtless put there to retard their advance. The Fourth Virginia Regiment was at this point in the front, and Captain Morgan Strother, its commander, when he discovered the barricade, ordered some of his men to dismount to remove the obstruction. While this was being done, he suddenly gave the order for the dismounted men to mount, which was immediately obeyed, and just then an incident occurred worthy of mention, as exhibiting a deed of individual heroism rarely witnessed. Just as the men of the Fourth Regiment were well in the saddle, after the order of their commanding officer, a single soldier, coming from the direction of the enemy, with sword in hand, dashed into the Black Horse Troop, which composed one of the squadrons of the Fourth Virginia Cavalry, and on that occasion was the color squadron, sabering the men right and left, wounding several, and among them Lientenant William A. Moss, and Corporal Hugh Hamilton, a gallant soldier and the color-bearer. The boldness and suddenness of the attack paralyzed for a moment or two the Confederates, and in that interval this bold assailant succeeded in forcing his way through the Confederate column, and might possibly have escaped, but a shot fired by a Confederate brought his horse down and he fell with it. He was at once surrounded and received a sabre cut in the face while in the act of parrying a blow from a carbine; another Confederate gave him a sabre thrust in the back, and in all probability he would have been slain on the spot but for the timely interference of Captain Henry C. Lee, an aid of Colonel Munford, who, seeing the struggle, rode up and put an end to it. It is said that Captain Lee recognized in the prostrate man a brother mason, through some sign or cry used by the masonic order in times of distress or danger. The hero of this affair, which sounds so like a romance, turned out to be Captain George N. Bliss, of the First Rhode Island Cavalry, at that time commanding the provost guard of General Torbert, who was in command of this force at Waynesboro. He was, of course, captured, and his explanation of his rash and desperate enterprise was, that he was, under the orders of Colonel Charles R. Lowell, Second Massachusetts Cavalry, leading a charge of a squadron of the Third New Jersey Cavalry, and that he did not discover, until among the enemy, that the squadron that had been following him at a charge had wheeled about and left him unsupported and alone, and that rather than surrender, he determined upon the bold project of attempting to break through the Confederate column and escape from the other side. It came near being a success, and at the same time his escape from death was almost a miracle. This adventure ended the work of the day. Immediately after it, Captain Strother advanced with his regiment, but found that the Union force had retreated, and, as it was now dark, pursuit was impracticable. Beyond driving the Union troops from Waynesboro and inflicting some damage, the results to the Confederates were not very important. By some mischance, General Breckenridge's division of infantry did not get up in time to intercept the Federal force on the Staunton road.

A. D. PAYNE,

Late Captain of the Black Horse Troop,
(Co. 4,) Fourth Virginia Cavalry,
C. S. A.

WARRENTON, VA.

APPENDIX. 85

I had always supposed my horse was killed, but in Richmond, Virginia, in May, 1880, I was introduced by Captain H. C. Lee to Captain H. C. Ballard, who said he was with dismounted cavalry, acting as sharpshooters that day, that himself and a dozen others fired at me, and that the bullet glanced along the skull at the burr of the ear, stunning him for a time, but that the horse soon recovered and did good service afterwards in the Fourth Virgina Cavalry of the Confederate army.

G N B.

LYNCHBURG, VA., March 4, 1882.

CAPTAIN GEORGE N BLISS, First Rhode Island Cavalry, late of U. S. A.:

DEAR SIR:—I am in receipt of your letter by this evening's mail, asking me to give you an account, from a Confederate standpoint, of the action on the 28th of September, 1864, at Waynesboro, Augusta county, Virginia, between the cavalry under my command and the Federal cavalry, commanded by General Torbert. I very much regret that I have no data at hand in the shape of a report from the commanding officers of either of the four regiments, or from Captain Johnston, commanding the battery attached to my brigade. So much time has elapsed since those scenes occurred, my memory cannot be trusted. Reading your narrative has recalled to my mind many points, but it is impossible for me to particularize lest I may do injustice to some of the noble and glorious spirits who so generously sustained me upon all occasions when their best efforts were required. My brigade was composed of the First, Second, Third and Fourth Virginia Cavalry, A. N. V., and Captain Johnston, of the Horse Artillery, with two guns, was serving with me that day, when we left our camp near Weyer's cave.

My orders from General Early, commanding the Valley District, were to move at once to Waynesboro, and attack the Federal cavalry who had gone there to cut the Chesapeake and Ohio Railroad and to destroy the iron bridge over the Shenandoah river between Waynesboro and the mouth of the tunnel at the Blue Ridge. I was notified that we would be supported by the infantry Having the advantage of a company in my command whose homes were in that county, (Captain McCluny, First Virginia Cavalry,) instead of taking the most direct road to

Waynesboro, which I knew was heavily picketed by the Federal cavalry, I secured a guide who carried me by a blind road through the "old coaling," along the foot-hills of the Blue Ridge, which had not been used for years, but with the assistance of a few axes we soon made it so that the artillery could accompany us; indeed, their indomitable spirit was such that they would go wherever we could go. Coming out by this blind road, where we were least expected, I found the Federal cavalry hard at work endeavoring to destroy the railroad bridge. I crossed the main road half a mile from the mouth of the tunnel which was guarded by a *malitia* force, consisting of the reserves from Staunton and Waynesboro, under Colonel Leo, but who had withdrawn to the top of the mountain. From this point I could see the Federal picket. Dismounting the First, Second and Third Regiments, I ordered the Fourth Regiment, Colonel William B. Wooldridge commanding, to charge this picket, mounted, and deploying the three dismounted regiments, moved rapidly to the attack. Captain Johnston's guns were pushed up at a swift trot to a commanding position and used most effectively. Perceiving that my attack from that unexpected quarter was a surprise, I was not slow to push my advantage, and pushing steadily forward, I drove the force from the bridge and saved it. Meeting a stout resistance at the river, where we lost some good men, I soon cleared my approach to it with my artillery, driving the Federals through the town of Waynesboro. General Early, by this time, had arrived with the infantry *via* regular road on the northwest of the town, and a few artillery shots from General John Pegram's command started General Torbert to change his base. I more than regret that I cannot here give a detailed account of this fight; no record has ever been made of it; we were so constantly engaged during those stirring times, no opportunity was afforded us for elaborate reports. I well remember the good services of Captain Henry C. Lee, A. & I. G; Major J W. Tayloe, A. A. A. G.; Rev. Randolph McKim, Chaplain of Second Regiment Regular Cavalry, acting A. D. C.; Colonel Cary Breckenridge, Second Virginia Cavalry; Colonel William B. Woolridge, Fourth Virginia Cavalry; Colonel W A. Morgan, First Virginia Cavalry, and Lieutenant-Colonel Field, Third Virginia Cavalry, were never wanting upon any field, and gave me their best efforts and support upon that occasion.

In fighting over our battles, as all good soldiers love to do with those who went hand in hand together, I have frequently had the incidents you recalled in your letter, mentioned by those of us who witnessed it, and it affords me pleasure to say it was worthy of a better support than you received from the ranking officer ordering the charge, or the men who should have followed. A little dare-deviltry in a cavalry officer sometimes acts like magic; a few dashing fellows, well led, have turned a victory from one side to a rout on the other, without any cause. As we are strangers, neither being able to recognize the other were we to meet, I can only say your courage will never be doubted by any Confederate who saw your manly bravery in the fight, and you may thank a kind Providence that you are now alive to tell your own story in your own way. You have spoken in a manly and generous way of what passed in our lines. When I saw you at night, sitting behind a Confederate cavalryman, with the blood streaming down your face, going to the rear, a prisoner, I said to Doctor Randolph, brigade surgeon, that you were one of the "widow's son party." He being one of the elder brothers, replied, "I'll see your mother's son well taken care of this night," and as most of the staff officers were of the clan, they did the best they could for a brother in trouble.

I am not a mason, but most of my staff were masons, and I know they frequently did many things that seemed to give them extra pleasure, for the unfortunate on the other side. I was sure the institution was full of good works, and, although I was only a poor soldier who tried to do his duty, without being a mason, I believed the organization was based upon Christian principles, and was always in sympathy with the work of the fraternity.

I can only add that every true and generous soldier, on either side, was willing to extend the healing balm to friend or foe, after the battle was over.

Thanking you for your kind letter, and wishing you prosperity, I am, with much respect,

THOMAS T. MUNFORD,
Brig.-Gen. Cav., A. N. V Late War.

P S.—Should you ever come to Lynchburg again, I should be glad to meet you, and if I can give you any information connected with the operations of our cavalry during the war, will do so with pleasure. I was four years with the Army of N. V

---

PORTLAND, ME., Dec. 16, 1879.

MY DEAR BLISS:—You ask me to give an account of my interview with Major Turner on the day you

APPENDIX. 91

were sent to the cells in the Libby. It was December 9, 1864; you came up from the hospital in the Libby, December 7, and it gave me much pleasure to greet an old college friend, even in such a place. During the following day, though we were interrupted by the visit of a committee of the Confederate Congress, who came to inquire into the condition of the prison, we recited our army experiences, and made ourselves as comfortable as the situation allowed. On Friday, December 9th, early in the forenoon, Captain Boice and Lieutenant Huff were sent to the cells. Not long after, Dick Turner came up stairs and called for Major Phillips, Lieutenant Towle and myself. Following him down stairs, we were shown into Major Turner's office, and were informed by the Major himself that we were to be sent to the cells and held as hostages for some men, bushwhackers, I inferred, who had been captured by our forces in the West, and sentenced to be hung. He then read an order from Commissioner Ould in reference to the matter.

Only a day or two before, I had found in a Richmond paper the following: "Roger A. Pryor has been set to Fort Lafayette. A Washington telegram says: 'Roger A. Pryor arrived here this morning and leaves to-night for Fort Lafayette. He attracted much attention as he was escorted down the avenue to the old Capitol, under guard, and was recognized by many of his former acquaintances here.' It is probable that he will soon be returned, as it is understood that Captain Burrage, for whose capture he was taken, in retaliation, is to be returned." I called the attention of Major Turner to this announcement, and remarked that I thought he was complicating matters. He said that the fact in reference to Pryor had escaped his attention, and added, "I cannot take you." Then he turned to his list and said, "I will take Captain ———, — Massachusetts Volunteers, the name I have forgotten; it was a German name, and Turner asked if the officer he had selected was American born. When informed that he was a German, he ran his eye again over his list, saying, "I must have a Massachusetts officer." But finding none, he turned to Dick Turner, and said, "Bring down Captain Bliss, First Rhode Island Cavalry." I went up stairs with a sad heart, but remember well the bold face you put on as you packed up your things and followed Dick Turner down stairs. There was nothing I would not have given could I have recalled the suggestion which secured my own release at your expense. I had only one more day at the Libby before I was sent with other prisoners to Danville, and we did not meet again until after the close of the war, but I was glad to learn that you were relieved and exchanged even before I was.

Always truly yours,<br>
Henry S. Burrage,<br>
Captain Thirty-sixth Massachusetts Volunteers.

P S.—The regiments of Captain Boice, Lieutenant Huff, Major Phillips and Lieutenant Towle I cannot give.

I enclose a scrap of paper which you sent to me during the first night, I think, you were in the cells; you sent it up by the officer of the guard. Upon the enclosed scrap of paper the following appears written with a lead pencil:

"Captain Burrage:—Please deliver my money to Lieutenant Adams, who will give it to me. We are all 5 in one cell, 8ft. by 12 ft.; the floor is of wood, raised about 12 inches above the ground; we have a fire, but find it cold nights. Tell Trippe, C. S., to send down the articles we sent out for. We do not know yet for whom we are held.

"Yours truly,<br>
"G. N. Bliss.

"P S.—We are all well.      G. N B."

BUCKINGHAM C. H., VA., June 21, 1884.

CAPTAIN GEORGE N BLISS, No. 2 College street, Providence, R. I. :

MY DEAR CAPTAIN :—I regret exceedingly that so much time has elapsed, and that I should have delayed you so much in your publication of the Waynesboro fight, but my time has not been my own, and I am a poor hand in the descriptive line, albeit it is about the late war, in which you and I took so active a part.

I think it was in the afternoon of the 28th day of September, 1864, when we first met; it has been so long my memory may fail me, and I have not visited the ground since the war, but I am sure I state the prominent facts. I made a charge with my squadron and met you with a regiment near a house on the right of the street, near the top of a hill, in Waynesboro. Your regiment came in good order until within one hundred yards of my command, when it deserted you with the exception of two men, who followed you. Your men had placed a barricade across the street which you and one of your men leaped, and at that point I engaged you with the sabre, and was at once put on the defensive by your superior swordsmanship, which kept me active to prevent a thrust from you. At this juncture

I received a pistol wound from the man who followed on your right, which so disabled me that I had to abandon the fight; my horse reared and plunged to the rear, my bridle hand being disabled by the wound referred to above, when you spurred up and struck me with your sabre on the back of the head; I tried to draw my pistol, but having my sabre knot over my wrist and being disabled in the bridle hand, I could not do so, and you passed me, striking two of my men just in front of me. Captain H. C. Lee has told me that he met you afterwards, and that you had requested him to give you his recollections of the affair. At this point my memory ceases until a later hour, about dark, when I became conscious and was in an ambulance, and some one said there was a "Yankee officer," badly wounded, and would I let him ride in the ambulance. I said, "Certainly, bring him in;" you took the seat with the driver, but becoming faint, said you must lie down; the surgeon had given me some apple brandy and I gave you some, which revived you, and we had a conversation which satisfied me that you were the officer who wounded me. My brother, Beverly T. Moss, now of Surry County, Virginia, who in that day's fight had gotten his leg shattered, but who, with unusual fortitude, had forgotten himself in his effort to take care of me, (I was shot through the left breast,) said he would go and give you some breakfast if his leg was well enough, and did hobble away, and came back and said you could not eat, and said if he could he would search the man out who had stolen your boots, but he was not able to walk.

I have stated little incidents connected with the Waynesboro fight, and will thank you to put me right where I may be in fault as to dates.

Very truly your friend,

W. A. Moss,

Late Captain Co. K, Fourth Virginia Cavalry.

---

114 West Grace Street,
Richmond, Va., July 20, 1884.

Captain George N. Bliss, Providence, R. I.:

My Dear Captain:—I found your letter of the 18th inst. here when I came up from the office last night, and in reply will say that it is so long since the event occurred that I can't give you many details. The war to me now is like a panorama. With us in the cavalry, marching night and day, as we

## APPENDIX.

were constantly doing, the events ran into each other, and it is hard to get hold of dates; but as you have kindly furnished me with this one, I shall begin, only hoping that Mrs. Bliss and the little Blisses may think I did right.

I was at that time, the 28th of September, 1864, the day of the fight at Waynesboro, Virginia, the Adjutant and Inspector-General of Wickham's Cavalry Brigade, Fitzhugh (Fitz.) Lee's Cavalry Division, Stuart's Cavalry Corps, Army of Northern Virginia. Our brigade was then composed of the First, Second, Third and Fourth Regiments of Virginia Cavalry, and we generally had a battery of Stuart's Horse Artillery with us; at that time I think we had Johnston's Battery of the S. H. A. As you have probably learned, our corps, divisions, brigades and batteries were called after their commanders. You tell me you have heard from some others of our command, and among them, General Munford, then the Colonel of the Second Regiment, so I shall merely begin at the fight. As you are probably aware, we were sent to prevent the destruction of the railroad bridge over the river, near Waynesboro, where the Virginia Central (now Chesapeake & Ohio) Railroad crossed. We were informed that you were destroying that bridge. From our marching on the blind road, on the side of the Blue Ridge Mountains, we were not very well closed up when we struck the turnpike, near Waynesboro, and it was from this fact that I had the opportunity of serving you. When we struck the turnpike we were between your forces and your pickets, which we captured, and you did not know of our coming. As we neared the town, our advanced guard reported a regiment of cavalry watering at the stream just east of the town. Orders were sent to our regiments to close up as rapidly as possible, but being strung out so badly, it was hard to do. Our order of marching was the order of regiments; thus, on one day the First Regiment would be in front, next the Second, next the Third, etc., and our horse artillery in rear, so you see if the First was in front the Fourth would be in the rear, and if the Fourth was in front the Third would be in the rear, the order of marching, Fourth, First, Second and Third and battery On this day the First was in front, and was dismounted and sent down the railroad; the Second and Third Regiments were also dismounted when they came up, and sent down the dirt road; the Fourth was sent forward mounted, and Johnston's Battery was placed on a knoll between the road and the railroad, from which point they did, as they generally did, some pretty good work. The first squadron of the Fourth, Captain Hill's, I think, was ordered to charge, which they did, gallantly, and some prisoners were taken by them, for I had the pleasure, having gone ahead with orders, of taking two of your men in this charge, for I needed a horse, but neither of them was worth much. This squadron was met with a volley from the enemy and were somewhat scattered; then the next squadron, Captain Moss's, was sent forward, and they charged up into the town; the remainder of the Fourth supported it. Just as Captain Moss got into town, owing to the Third not being up, and the Second not well in position, I was sent forward by Colonel Munford, who was then commanding our brigade, to halt the squadron of the Fourth, and as I was galloping up one side (the right) of these squadrons, (we were in column of fours) I saw you galloping down on the other side. Knowing you would be looked after, particularly as you were alone, I kept on and halted the head of the troops, and then I saw your men going in the opposite direction; these are the ones you told me, when I first saw you after the war, you expected to lead in the charge against us, and thought were following you, I think you called them the "Butterflies." My orders were also to bring our troops back that had been sent up on the road to the right, the First Regiment, for we were nearly into Sheridan's camp, and were fearful that your troops might sweep down this street and cut this party off, and it was as I was returning and had gotten to this corner, that I saw your horse fall, and three or four of our men with you. As I passed you, you called out for relief as a mason, and making a sign which I recognized, I ordered our men to let you alone, take you to the rear and see that you were attended to, as you seemed to be wounded. I had to go on to bring our troops back and, although you said something to me, I had no time to stop. One of our men was about to kill you when I got to you, and informed me that you had badly wounded Captain Moss, and had struck somebody else, I have forgotten now who, and thought it was wrong for me to interfere. When I came back, of course you were gone, and the horse too, I think, and I never saw you again until you came down to see me here in 1880. I heard that you and Captain Moss were carried back in the same ambulance, and Moss, having some "apple-jack," our national drink, you took a drink together The next I heard of you, you had been sent to Richmond. I did not have an opportunity of seeing you when you were sent to the rear.

I was tired, besides I had been struck on the inside of the right leg by a carbine ball and had my horse wounded at the same time, when your men fired from the creek, and my leg was sore. My horse was a fine grey one, and captured from your people by one of Moseby's men, and I got him from him. After he was struck he bled pretty freely; the ball struck him in the right front shoulder, just above his U. S. mark. As I rode back on the knoll, where the artillery was, Lieutenant Willie Hoxton, of the S. H. A., seeing the parts torn from my leg where I had been struck, thought the horse's blood was mine. I shall never forget the look on his young and handsome face when he asked me if I had been that badly hurt, and the relief he seemed to feel when I showed him where the horse was struck. This horse was afterwards shot in one of the skirmishes on the retreat from Richmond, when I was riding him. I sent him back to the wagon train. There he was captured by your cavalry in some dash on the train. I was sorry to lose "Pip," which had been with me in some right tight places. I would have liked to have had him in peace, instead of the miserable glass-eyed little Yankee pony on which I was paroled. Neither of the horses I got at Waynesboro were worth much. I turned one over with the prisoners, and had one kept for me, a large iron grey, which I afterwards traded off with one of our division headquarters couriers, and got a right good horse in return. I enclose you a memorandum of Major W F Graves, (who commanded the Second Regiment at that time), written last winter, when he was here as a member of the legislature. May be this will be of service to you. I made this a "heap" longer than I intended when I sat down. You can cull out from it what you want. With kind regards to Mrs. Bliss and yourself, from Mrs. Lee and myself, I am,

Very truly yours,<br>
HENRY C. LEE.<br>
Late Captain and A. A. and I. G. P A. C. S.

## Major W F Graves' Memorandum.

At the battle of Waynesboro, on September 28, 1864, the Second Regiment of Virginia Cavalry was dismounted and took position on a ridge just to the left of the turnpike leading from Charlottesville to Waynesboro, said ridge overlooking said town. When the charge was made by the Confederate forces, the Second Regiment pushed forward, supported by the Fourth Regiment, Virginia Cavalry, which was mounted, driving the enemy back. When the Federal forces fell back, there was a Federal quartermaster, by the name of Bliss, who volunteered to lead a charge to counteract the advance of the Confederate cavalry. The charge was made by the said officer solitary and alone, without his companions following and supporting him, cutting right and left with his sabre, until he reached a point, as well as I can remember, near the centre of the town, when his horse was shot down. Several Confederate soldiers had their guns and pistols raised to fire upon said officer, when he gave the masonic sign of distress, which was recognized by Captain Henry C. Lee, as he was a free mason, thus saving the life of as brave a soldier as ever drew a sabre in the Federal cavalry. I was an eye witness to the foregoing, and was not more than fifteen or twenty paces from him when his horse was shot down.

www.ingramcontent.com/pod-product-compliance
Lightning Source LLC
Chambersburg PA
CBHW020155170426

43199CB00010B/1056